♡
Debbie G. Harman.
2002

To Courtney—
"Merry Christmas"
2002
With lots of love,
Uncle Duane,
Aunt Lori &
family

Jesus Said . . .

Cover and interior design copyrighted 2002 by Covenant Communications, Inc.

Published by Covenant Communications, Inc.
American Fork, Utah

Printed in China
First Printing: September 2002

08 07 06 05 04 03 02   10 9 8 7 6 5 4 3 2 1

ISBN 1-59156-091-8

Jesus Said . . .

by Debbie G. Harman

Jesus said . . .

Come, follow me.

Our Father who art in Heaven, hallowed be thy name

For thine is the Kingdom, and the power, and the glory forever, Amen

For thine is the Kingdom, and the power, and the glory, forever, Amen

Our Father who art in Heaven, hallowed be thy name

Jesus said . . .

Pray unto the Father.

Jesus said . . .

Keep my commandments.

Jesus said . . .

...if planted, it will grow. ♥

faith is like a little seed....

In Loving Memory

Have faith in me.

This is my **BELOVED Son**
in whom I am well **PLEASED**

Jesus said . . .

WE BELIEVE the first principles and
ordinances of the Gospel are

Faith

Baptism

Mice Rule

Repentance

Holy Ghost

Be baptized in my name.

Jesus said . . . . blessed are the m

k for they shall inherit the earth.

Jesus said . . .

Love one another.

Jesus said . . .

every man according to that which he hath, such as feeding the hungry, clothing the naked, visiting I would that ye should impart of your substance to the poor

the sick and administering to their relief, both spiritually and temporally, according to their ... wants

SCOUTING FOR FOOD

Free Apples

SOUP

I was an hungred, and
ye gave me meat.

Jesus said . . .

I was sick and ye visited me.

Jesus said . . .

Inasmuch as ye have done this . . .
ye have done it unto me.

Jesus said . . .

Feed my sheep.

Jesus said . . . Except ye become as little chilo

, ye shall not enter into the kingdom of heaven.

Jesus said . . . this do

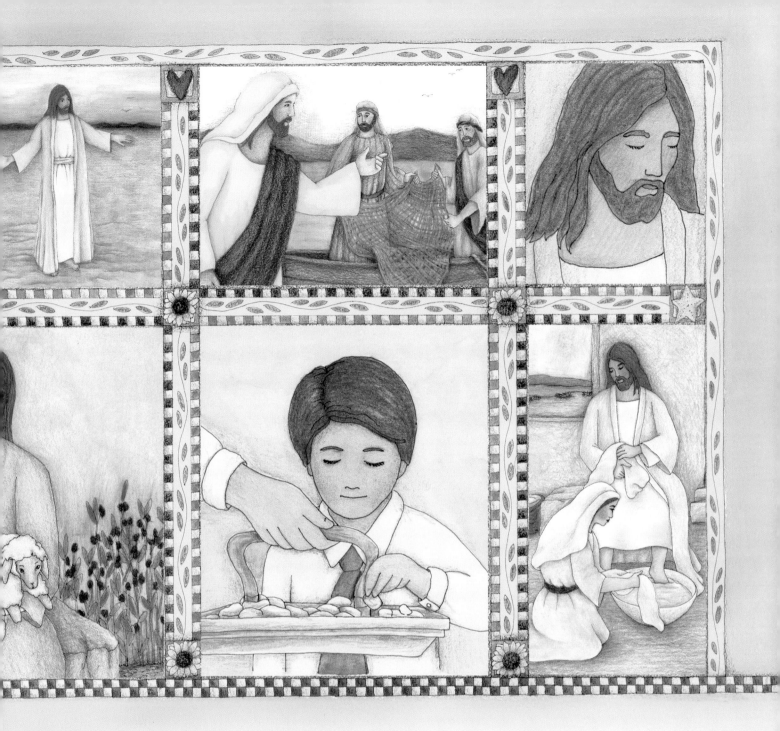

remembrance of me.

Jesus said . . .

I am the way, the truth, and the life.

Jesus said . . .
in me there is
no end.